Why Do I Have To Die?

David Allan Hubbard

G/L
REGAL
BOOKS™

A Division of G/L Publications
Glendale, California, U.S.A.

Other good Regal reading by David Allan Hubbard
Church—Who Needs It?
Is Life Really Worth Living?
What's God Been Doing All This Time?
Will We Ever Catch Up with the Bible?

Scripture quotations in this publication are from the *Revised Standard Version* of the Bible, copyrighted 1946 and 1952 by the Division of Christian Education of the NCCC, U.S.A., and used by permission.

Published by Regal Books Division, G/L Publications
Glendale, California 91209
Printed in U.S.A.

Library of Congress Catalog Card No. 77-020572
ISBN 0-8307-0618-6

Contents

Contents

Introduction

Part of my research for this book included a number of conversations with Dr. Neil Warren, dean of the School of Psychology at Fuller Theological Seminary. A sensitive Christian, as well as a skilled therapist and counselor, Dr. Warren has made death and dying an area of special interest. He has gained helpful insights into the implications of dying and how it affects the human spirit and the human life.

Following is a compilation of remarks which Dr. Warren and I exchanged on the subject of death and dying.

Dr. Hubbard: Our society seems fascinated with death. Why is that?

Dr. Warren: As a society, I think we are painfully confused about how to handle death. On the one hand we deny it every chance we get. On the other hand we can't get enough of it. The movies we go to indicate this: *Towering Inferno, Jaws, Earthquake, Poseidon Adventure.* Television is filled with death every week—hundreds of people, thousands of people dying. One man, Mark Golden, who was formerly in charge of program development at CBS said, "There is one constant in every dramatic TV story form and that is that the leading character's occupation is somehow connected with death." He says, "I don't know why, but story forms connected with death are the only ones that home audiences are willing to watch in numbers large enough to make a dramatic series economically viable."[1]

Dr. Hubbard: What would be your interpretation, psychologically, of this fascination with death?

Dr. Warren: Largely, I think it's because we try to keep death at a distance, to keep it impersonal. As long as death happens in unnatural ways to unreal people out there somewhere, we don't have to get personally involved. I am convinced that if we could help one another face our own deaths squarely enough, the violence and destructiveness of our society could be reduced significantly.

Dr. Hubbard: That leads us to the deeper and more

personal question—why do we fear death so much?

Dr. Warren: Dr. Robert Neale[2] in New York City has devised a questionnaire designed to help us get hold of what it is we fear about death. He says that some of us fear what will happen after death. We are concerned about the fate of our bodies or about the judgment or about the unknown out there. Some of us fear the process of dying, the pain we think we are going to experience, the indignity that perhaps we will go through, the burden our experience will bring to those we love. But most of us fear the loss of life, that is, the loss of mastery that we have developed painfully, slowly, over time, the incompleteness we may experience at the time of our death, the separation, of course, from our loved ones and those things we have grown to appreciate so much about life.

Many people in our society have never really learned to live fully. Their faith is not big enough to handle the potency of the death experience. "Death is the one event in my life," one person said, "which confronts me with the question of the meaning and purpose of life and the significance of the future." That's a lot we have to face and it takes a big faith to handle a big experience like death.

Dr. Hubbard: Is there a correlation between how we live and how we die?

Dr. Warren: Research evidence is clear on that. Persons who learn to live fully, who really know how to experience life in the moment, die much more

7

meaningfully than persons who never learn to get into the moment. The fact seems to be that if we can appropriate our faith enough so that we can experience God's love in every moment and allow ourselves to take the risks that are required in living our lives, we will approach death much more ready to move on through that difficult experience.

Dr. Hubbard: So the key is a deep personal faith that takes God's love seriously?

Dr. Warren: That's exactly true. Our research says that those individuals who have a logical cognitive faith that stays only in their heads have a great deal of difficulty when it comes to facing up to death. But those individuals who have a logical and cognitive faith but allow it to move right down into their bones and muscles, so that it really changes them from within, come to death much more ready to move through that experience.

Dr. Hubbard: Does this mean then, that there is actual psychological evidence that Christians may face death differently than others?

Dr. Warren: Whether Christians face death more effectively than non-Christians has been a burning issue among researchers for a number of years. The research results until lately have been contradictory and difficult to understand. But our latest research indicates that those individuals whose faith is intrinsic (internal, down inside of them) have far less death-anxiety and are much more willing to talk about the issues of death than those individuals whose faith is extrinsic, who use their faith to gain some kind of special advantage over life.

Dr. Hubbard: How would a psychologist go about discovering intrinsic or extrinsic faith? Are there tests or instruments or questionnaires? How would you come to that kind of conclusion?

Dr. Warren: There has been a lot of time spent in developing tests like these. Gordon Allport at Harvard University developed a test called the Eiro Scale, the extrinsic/intrinsic religious orientation scale which helps us look much more precisely at what religious faith, Christian faith is.

Dr. Hubbard: Using Dr. Allport's scale, does your research support the idea that we are able to face death more positively—be less torn up, less anxious, less threatened by the whole thing—if we have a deep basic commitment of faith and trust? If we are more accepting of the fact that death will be a peaceful transition, a doorway into another life?

Dr. Warren: Yes it does. It seems to be the case that if we can keep life and death in a healthy tension so that we can recognize how powerful death is for us, and also develop a faith that is big enough to handle that powerful experience, we can gain energy to relate more effectively to our life. At the same time we can gain certainty out of life that allows us to approach death with confidence.

Dr. Hubbard: As Jesus was dying He said, "Father,

into your hands I commend my spirit."[3] Is this the kind of faith and joyful resignation we want to have when we face our own dying?

Dr. Warren: I think when we experience the love God has for us deep within ourselves we can have that kind of acceptance.

Dr. Hubbard: Many of our readers may be close to death or are facing death in the experience of their loved ones. They have aged parents or grandparents; they know the family circle is going to be sundered temporarily by death; they know they are going to pass through that grief. Yet many of our readers also know the hope of Christ's resurrection and the joy of what lies beyond death. How do we get these together? How can our Christian hope help us as our families go through these experiences?

Dr. Warren: Incorporating the hope of the resurrection into the lives of our families seems to be the crucial matter. There are some things families can do that help them get hold of that hope. One of the things families need to do at the time of a death is to sit down together and do a lot of talking and communicating. Sometimes, as families, we become fragmented and we haven't communicated as deeply to one another our own feelings about one another as we need to do, and death often gives us that opportunity. One of the things that will happen in that conversation, I suspect, is that we will begin to experience the diversity of family response to that person

10

who has died. We need to recognize that diversity will be there, and to prize it as we talk together.

Dr. Hubbard: You mean some people may weep a good bit, others may not. People may express and feel their grief different ways, is that what you mean?

Dr. Warren: That's exactly right. Some of us will be very unsettled, maybe even angry. Our loved one has gone ahead and died and we maybe feel abandoned. Others of us will feel all right about it, that this is the right time for this to have happened. But all of those feelings should be allowed and prized in the family group. Something else I have found important as I have worked with families who have had someone die within their group is to remember the one who has died and the role he played in the family life from as many different perspectives as possible. Like when we are able to cry together as a family and also to laugh about that one who has died, to remember his successes and his attributes while, at the same time, remembering some times when perhaps he wasn't so successful.

Dr. Hubbard: Is there just one more word you would have for us on this?

Dr. Warren: Just two quick words; one is that, as a family, we need to explore the future and what it may hold for our family unit now that one has left us. Sometimes this means we need to rearrange our priorities, to pick up some of the responsibilities this person had.

The last thing would be that, as a family group, we need to reaffirm individual commitment to the family and family commitment to every individual member. We want to use the death experience as a great springboard to help us as a family to move more effectively into life.

Dr. Hubbard: So out of death comes strength and love. Surely this is God's will: that His joy and hope will strengthen our love in those trying moments.

Notes

1. Marc Golden, quoted by Sam Blum in "Who Decides What Gets on TV and Why," *New York Times* Magazine, (September 3, 1967).
2. Dr. Robert Neale, Professor of psychology and religion at the Union Theological Seminary, New York, in his book, *The Art of Dying* (New York: Harper and Row Publishers, Inc., 1973).
3. See Luke 23:46.

12

1. Why Do I Have to Die?

*The Lord God took the man and put him in the
garden of Eden to till it and keep it. And the
Lord God commanded the man, saying, "You
may freely eat of every tree of the garden; but of
the tree of the knowledge of good and evil you
shall not eat, for in the day that you eat of it you
shall die."*   **Genesis 2:15-17**

The first mention of it can spoil almost any party.
Like a wet blanket on a wintry day, like ice
cubes down the shirt-front, talk of dying can chill any
conversation to a shivering silence.

13

We can discuss tragedies like earthquakes, train wrecks or plane crashes with a certain detached dismay. We can converse about crimes like bombings, kidnappings and hijackings with a remote involvement. But let the talk turn to the matter of our dying and voices choke, faces pale, palms grow sweaty.

Strange it is that an experience toward which all of us are heading should leave us speechless. The circumstances of our birth and early upbringing we reflect upon with nostalgia. The events of our schooling we freely share with the wistfulness of an old friendship. The ups and downs of marital adjustment and family raising we can chronicle with the proper mix of joy and sobriety. But the fact that we will die—that is scarcely fit material for discussion. My own pen seems to stutter with some reluctance as I write these words.

We are at war with ourselves over this topic. The passing of time tells us that our bodies are pressing toward frailty. We take longer to stoop to pick up the newspaper and stand up again with caution to ease the kinks. Then we hold the paper further from our tiring eyes to bring it into focus. After that we remember less of what we just read than once we did. The morning paper becomes a symbol of our aging, especially when we sadly spot the name of an old acquaintance in the obituary column.

But protesting against the taxes that the years have levied is a youthful, fighting spirit whose motto is

14

"never say die." We look at the mirror and find it hard to believe what we see. Grey at the temples and wrinkled under the eyes, we say, "That must be someone else. I feel much younger than that."

Something there is within the human spirit that resists the idea of dying. This is true for all of us, and especially for those who have entered that intimate relationship with God that the Bible calls eternal life. So rich is that fellowship, so bright that vitality, so refreshing that change, that we find it hard to accept the fact of death.

Why do I have to *die*? is a basic query that wells up from the depths of our being. Why do *I* have to die? is the form the question takes.

The answers are not easy. Not easy because the questions touch so painfully on a subject that we find disturbing. And not easy because the how, why, and what of death bring us to the edge of mystery. Nowhere does our human nearsightedness annoy us more than when we stand at the brink of this mystery and try to peer into its obscure depths.

Why do I have to die? The light with which the Bible illuminates that puzzle is not as bright as we would wish but it is bright enough to help us discern some facets of the question that nothing else could rescue from the shadows. When we lean forward and peer at the matter, blinking to adjust to the Bible's light, what comes into focus behind the question of death is the figure of God. There can be no insight to the subject of dying that is not insight to the nature of God—the God who creates, the God who judges, the God who conquers.

God Is the Creator; I Am the Creature

"In the beginning God..." so the first words of the Bible read. "In the end God..." is the way we might paraphrase the last pages of the Bible, the book of the Revelation. When we open the Bible God is already there; when we close it He is as much alive and as much at work as when the story began. Here is one way He has described Himself: "'I am the Alpha and the Omega,' says the Lord God, who is and who was and who is to come, the Almighty" (Rev. 1:8).

What does all this have to do with death? Just this: our dying is part of the difference between us and God. Everything living on earth is destined to die. From the oldest redwood tree to the smallest microbe, all God's earthly creations are mortal. I am one of them. God is the Creator; I am His creature.

As a creature my life is derived from God. I have no capacity to originate life or to sustain it. From its beginning to its end, my life is a gift. Only the Creator is *living* in the fullest sense. Only He has life in Himself; only He needs no life from outside Himself; only He is not subject to death. He is self-contained, without beginning or end. He is the Alpha and Omega, the A and the Z—indeed, the whole alphabet. Compared with Him, we are broken letters that

16

arrive lately and depart early, leaving all life's messages incomplete.

I am different from God. Whatever else I can say about dying, it is the firm, the persistent reminder that I am different from God—not by a little but by a whole lot, by the difference between life and death. I need to remember this because my arrogance and my wishful thinking often blind me to the realities of His majesty and my limits.

As a creature, my life is dependent on God. His grace and power provide the bread for my body and the breath for my existence. He is the atmosphere in which "we live and move and have our being" (Acts 17:28). Without Him I have no existence, whether I know it or not.

Why do I have to die? That is a vexing, gnawing question. I would rather not have to raise it. Yet it keeps bubbling up within me as I look at thinning temples and speckled hands, the sure signs of creeping age. One way I can live with the question is to let it drive me to God. The fact that I will die can lead me to cling to God who alone has and gives life. It is no bad thing to be a creature; it is only bad to be a creature who does not love and trust the Creator. The reality of death—painful though it be—can be a spur to help me with that love and trust.

God Is the Judge; I Am the Rebel

Death is mentioned early in the Bible, not long

after the first descriptions of life: "The Lord God took the man and put him in the garden of Eden to till it and keep it. And the Lord God commanded the man, saying, 'You may freely eat of every tree of the garden; but of the tree of the knowledge of good and evil you shall not eat, for in the day that you eat of it you shall die'" (Gen. 2:15-17).

These words clearly connect human death with divine punishment for disobedience. What is not so clear is how that connection should be understood. Would the human family have died had they not rebelled against God's authority? We cannot know for sure. The best guess is that we, like all other creatures, were created mortal. One argument for this is that without death the earth would be overrun, swamped with living creatures, ever breeding and never dying.

The words of God to Adam carry a double emphasis. They speak of the *fact of death,* and they mention the *time of death:* "For in the day that you eat of it you shall die." It seems likely that what God was saying was that disobedience would bring an instant change in man's relationship to Him—a change that would separate man from God who was the source of his life. That separation marked the beginning of a process of judgment which would lead to death.

History shows that such judgment actually took place. The rebel man and woman were banished from the garden and wandered toward their inevitable death, alienated from fellowship with God. From that time on, the last line of everyone's biography has read "and he died." Genesis 5 tolls out that phrase like a funeral knell for all the sons of Adam except Enoch, of whom it is said: "Enoch walked with God; and he was not, for God took him" (Gen. 5:24).

Whether there would have been death without sin we cannot say. What is clear is that this side of our human rebellion, death, has taken on the character of punishment. It is a constant reminder that God is the judge and that I am a rebel.

Why do I have to die? That question has a rather stern answer in the pages of the Bible. I have to die because I am part of a human family that foolishly and wickedly rebelled against God and is subject to His judgment. Can I really face that question? Can I let the reality of death as judgment lead me to come to terms with the judge? If so, the thought of death will have done one of its duties—it will have prompted me to seek God's grace before I die.

God Is the Conqueror; Death Is the Victim

When we human beings look at death, we must always see God standing behind it. Our death may resemble the death of a plant or an animal in its physical symptoms: cessation of life, failure of the metabolism to function, rapid deterioration of the body. But we are more than animals. For this reason the question "Why do I have to die?" goads us so.

19

Our dying is not just part of a natural cycle; our existence is not merely an example of how the fit survive. Death has to do with our relationship to God; because we are made by Him, death has more than passing significance. It is not just an act of nature, like the wilting of a flower or the falling of a leaf. It is an enemy—the last enemy, Paul called it.

Yet it is a conquered enemy. God is the conqueror; death is His victim. He who promised death as judgment to the rebels set Himself to deal with that very judgment.

God the Son went through the experience of death with us and for us. The pain, the anxiety, the uncertainty, the dread of death were all experiences that He understood. By His death He has robbed death of some of its strangeness; by His resurrection He has loosed it of its power.

Why do I have to die? That is not a pretty question. We are not tempted to sing a song, write a poem, or paint a poster featuring it. But we can handle it, as we let that question draw us to the God who stands behind it. He is the One who looms larger than death—the Creator on whom we depend, the Judge before whom we repent, the Conqueror to whom we cling in loving trust. Asking basic questions about death can lead us to fresh meaning for life.

2. What Will I Go Through When I Die?

Save me, O God! For the waters have come up to my neck. I sink in deep mire, where there is no foothold; I have come into deep waters, and the flood sweeps over me. I am weary with my crying; my throat is parched. My eyes grow dim with waiting for my God. **Psalm 69:1-3**

We had talked about death before, my mother and I. We had talked about it three years before when my father died. A surprising, a triumphant home-going his had been. He had finished a sermon on the love of God, closed his Bible, excused himself to the congregation, lain down on the platform beside the pulpit and died.

We had talked about death just a year later, when Ruth's and my baby son died after eight weeks of struggling existence.

Now mother and I were talking about death again. But this time our talk was different; it was mother who was dying. With her customary courage she had sailed to England to see Ruth and me, and to meet Mary, who was just two months old. Sick all the way on the ship, she arrived in England weak and jaundiced. The doctor's face was grave as he told me that he wanted to consult with a specialist. His suspicions were confirmed by the other doctor—cancer too far developed to allow surgery or any other treatment.

We Pass Through Various Stages

The stages that my mother went through in coming to terms with the news of her death were quite typical, though at the time I had had no other experiences with which to compare them. We face death as persons, not as textbook cases, so no two people die exactly alike. But there are similarities and patterns in the stages we go through, as Dr. Elisabeth Kübler-Ross has pointed out in her widely read book, *On Death and Dying.*[1] Dr. Kübler-Ross describes five stages a person encounters who discovers he or she is going to die.

The first stage is denial and isolation. "But the Lord has shown me that there will be a great revival and that I will be part of it" was among the first responses

22

my mother made when I talked with her about the cancer. This was her form of denial and isolation. Death could not happen to her, not at that time. Her work was not yet done; her faith that God had mighty works to perform was not yet vindicated. There must be some mistake. The Lord had not prepared her for this kind of news; she was not about to accept my statement or that of the two doctors as the last word.

The second milestone on the way to dying is anger. "Pray that the Lord will intervene" was her request to me and the friend with whom we were staying near London. The fire of indignation burned in her black eyes which seemed to gleam more brightly against the yellow of her jaundiced face. When we could only pray that the Lord's will be done, she seemed to direct a quiet scorn toward us. "O ye of little faith" was the message I read in her speechless stare. Let down she seemed to feel by her Lord, by her son, and by her friend. Anger was her reaction, though she resolutely kept it under control.

Bargaining is supposed to be the third stage according to Kübler-Ross. My memory is silent, after more than 20 years, as to whether my mother engaged in this. If so, it undoubtedly had a theological turn. It was not bargaining to have more time with friends or family. It would have been bargaining to complete her mission as Bible teacher and prayer warrior. Indeed, her desire to live to see revival sweep her church, her nation, the world may have expressed itself to God in a kind of bargaining. It would not at all have been beyond her, familiar as she was with the biblical example of bargaining for longer life by good king Hezekiah (see Isa. 38).

*The last two stages in our pilgrim path toward death—depression and acceptance—*are somewhat hard to distinguish in the few days I had with my mother. She went through periods of sleeping much and saying little, which I might diagnose as depression. Yet at the same time there was a noble resignation akin to that of a general asked to render up his sword upon retirement. For more than half a century she had been taking orders from above. Her Christian reflexes were highly military and they prompted her to silent surrender. But only hints of this were verbalized, possibly because the particular location of her cancer—liver and pancreas—formed its own anesthetic.

The conversations and impressions I have shared took place within the short span of three days. Then I put her on a plane to California. There she died peacefully a week or so later. My sister Laura, who tended her and cared for her affairs as death approached, has reported the signs of mother's quiet acceptance of her dying. She willingly and knowingly signed the papers that gave Laura power of attorney over her affairs. More than that, she firmly and graciously said no when some of her old friends wanted to come and pray for her recovery.

If these, then, are the stages through which many persons, including my mother, have passed on the journey to the other world, what can we say to help us face them? What words about God will give us hope and courage as we make that final transition?

Three things at least can be affirmed. First, God knows about these stages; in fact, as our Maker, He may well have planned them to help us through the difficult time. Second, God understands our emotions as we face death; then, as always, He wants us to tell Him how we feel. Third, God goes through the stages with us; no experience that touches us, no attitude that we muster can force Him from our side.

God Knows What We Go Through

To the one who is dying, and to the immediate family who share the experience, death is a drama for which there has been no rehearsal. It plays itself out on an unfamiliar stage, usually a hospital with its hushed conversations, its antiseptic smells, and its forbidding equipment. The players in the drama are a strange crew, clad in white or green, sometimes mysteriously masked, usually brusque and professional. Their vocabulary is weighted with technical terms like infarction and carcinoma or with shorthand like I.V., c.c.s., or stat.

And our responses are equally strange. One moment we look death in the eye and think we are ready for it. The next moment we change the subject and thrust death as far to the edges of our thought as possible.

We become confused in our attitudes and testy with the staff that cares for us and even with our own loved ones. And afterwards we are over-whelmed with our own weakness and failure. What a time that is to remember what God is like! Nothing that we go through is a surprise to Him.

God made us as we are. The various mechanisms like denial, anger, and bargaining are all part of the protective equipment He has built into our human personalities to help us handle death. He knows what we go through; He planned it that way. Our last enemy needs dealing with; God saw to it that we would be equipped for the task. Death does not frighten God away as it may some of our timid friends.

God cares for us as we are. Jesus' words about the sparrows need to be etched on the wall over our hospital beds:

> "Are not two sparrows sold for a penny?
>   And not one of them will fall
>   to the ground without your Father's will.
>   But even the hairs of your head
>   are all numbered.
>   Fear not, therefore; you are of more value
>   than many sparrows.
> (Matt. 10:29-31)

God Understands What We Feel

Dying may carry pain. Modern medication can help with some of that. But dying always carries heavy emotions. The anger we feel at the thought of going before we are ready, the grief of separation from those we shall leave behind, the uncertainty about the future—these and other emotions may swamp us.

When they do we may feel abandoned by those who do not seem to understand, or we may suffer guilt over the intensity of our feelings. What a time to remember what God is like! The Bible that He inspired is full of strong feelings. God not only understands them, He put them there for our good.

Listen to the cries of one sufferer whose words God was pleased to record:

Save me, O God!
For the waters have come
up to my neck.
I sink in deep mire,
where there is no foothold;
I have come into deep waters,
and the flood sweeps over me.
I am weary with my crying;
my throat is parched.
My eyes grow dim
with waiting for my God.
(Ps. 69:1-3)

Many persons at the door of death can identify

27

with those emotions. Deep water is a frequent metaphor for the suffering that may precede death. Fatiguing tears, parched throat, and dimming vision are all too familiar companions of pending death.

God has encouraged us to express our feelings. Who made our tear ducts? Who formed our sympathetic nervous system? Who shaped the glands that help to regulate our moods? God the personal Creator knew full well how deeply persons can be touched and grieved, and He saw to it that human persons had the means available to vent their emotions before they exploded.

He has offered to be our Father. What is that but an invitation to tell Him our problems? Is there any point to hiding from Him what He already knows? Nothing makes better sense as we pass through the stages of our dying than to tell God the Creator, God the Father, whatever we are feeling in the kaleidoscopic emotions that dying engenders.

God has experienced many of the feelings we express. The cross of Jesus is never far from our beds of illness. It sheds its light by day and night whenever God's people face death. It has many messages— peace, forgiveness, love, reconciliation. It also speaks of understanding. It reminds us that God the Son went through death's doors before us. His words from the cross—words of abandonment, words of thirst—show us how deeply He experienced our own emotions. We can count on God's understanding. The deep, dark feelings that pending death engenders are not foreign to Him.

God Goes with Us
Through the Stages of Dying

What will I go through when I die? For some of us that question is more pressing than for others. For all of us it is real and vital. That is why it is important for us to have some understanding of the stages that many persons go through when they receive the verdict that death is within sight.

What is more important is for us to know that God will go with us through every stage of our dying. His promises assure us of this. He has pledged Himself not to leave us or to forsake us. Death itself cannot make Him break that promise.

If we deny the thought of our death, He is there gently to help us face its reality. If we bubble over in anger at the outrage of our dying at this inopportune time, He will embrace us in His love as our resentment outpours. If we seek to bargain, He will quietly hear our terms and help us yield to His will. If we sink into sharp depression, He will wait by our side with soft words of love and comfort. As we accept the final reality of death, He will remind us that it is real but not final and will escort us to His own side in the world to come.

During my mother's last days, Laura asked her if she would like to hear some words from Scripture.

Her answer was a somewhat surprising—*No*. She had done her homework earlier. She knew where she was going and with whom. Fifty years she had spent in increasingly intimate acquaintance with the Lord of the Bible. Ahead of time she had partaken of the spiritual resources that would see her through. She felt no need to cram for her finals.

Footnote

1. Elisabeth Kübler-Ross, *On Death and Dying* (New York: The Macmillan Company, 1969).

3. How Can Others Help Me When My Time Comes?

Blessed be the God and Father of our Lord Jesus Christ, the Father of mercies and God of all comfort, who comforts us in all our affliction, so that we may be able to comfort those who are in any affliction, with the comfort with which we ourselves are comforted by God. For as we share abundantly in Christ's sufferings, so through Christ we share abundantly in comfort too. If we are afflicted, it is for your comfort and salvation; and if we are comforted, it is for your comfort, which you experience when you patiently endure the same sufferings that we suffer. Our hope for you is unshaken; for we know that as you share in our sufferings, you will also share in our comfort. 2 Corinthians 1:3-7

31

The phone call usually sounds something like this: "Sorry to hear that you have been so sick. I hate to think of you tied to that bed. It must be hard to accept when you have been so active. Is there anything I can do? Please let me know how I can help."

Chances are the phone call is followed by flowers and a cheery card. From some people that may be the extent of it. They have paid their courtesies, made their offer of help, and their consciences are clear. They have done what protocol requires, and now they can get on with their own pursuits.

Still the matter remains: when we are ill, especially ill unto death, we do need help. But we do not want that help from just anyone who may offer. Illness makes us weak and vulnerable. It is a time of intense privacy. We do not want our needs on display to people who do not care deeply.

How can others help me when my time comes? That is a crucial question both to a sufferer and to those who may surround him or her. Two simple questions flow out of our topic. First, who can help us best? Second, how can they help us best? No simple answers are in order, just some suggestions that will bring a practical and a biblical perspective to our needs.

Who Can Help Us Best?

When the phone call offers help, all kinds of things go through the mind. Do I really need help? Am I indeed coming to the point of such helplessness that I must depend much more on others? Those are not easy questions to accept, let alone to resolve. It takes a good bit of grace, an ample dose of humility, and a large measure of realism to say, "Yes, I am more dependent than I once was. I would appreciate some help."

But even when we cross that line, the questions do not stop. They may begin to focus not on our need but on the suitability of the other person's help. Is he someone reliable enough to count on? Do we know her well enough to feel comfortable with the more intimate relationship that her helping will thrust us into? With all that he has to do, can I possibly encroach on his time with my needs?

Who can help us best?

One obvious answer may be *those who are willing.* Unwilling helpers do not do very well. They trip over their feelings and mess up the carpet with their unresolved conflicts. Sometimes we have to take people at face value when they offer to help, but before long we can pick up clues—and none too subtle ones— that indicate the reluctance with which they help. If there are others available, we will be better off to excuse them graciously from their obligation and send them on their way.

Who can help us best?

Those who are closest to us is another part of the answer. No one can take the place of family members and old friends when our energies are low, our feelings are confused, and our spirits are depressed. A beloved colleague of mine once said, "We all need those with whom we can be weak." That is not a bad definition of intimacy. Our closest friends are those with whom we can be weak. And how we need them when we face death.

Preparing for death is something we should give more thought to. It probably should influence our early decisions more than it does. I have always admired a college friend who had the courage to break up with a boyfriend with whom she had gone steady for months. "I could not imagine myself sitting before the fire and rocking with him 50 years from now," was what she answered when I asked what had happened. She took the long view. She wanted a husband who would be not only fun in youth but a companion in old age.

Would we raise our children more effectively if we had our dying as well as our living in view? Would we demonstrate more compassion and tenderness, more caring and concern, if we remembered that we were training them for our own sake as well as theirs? The quality of thoughtfulness we have instilled in them is what they will demonstrate toward us.

The law of sowing and reaping which the Bible so often stresses has an application here. If we sow deep and loving ties with friends and family, those ties will moor us securely as the time of our departure comes to hand. The choice of friends might have one eye on dying—ours and theirs. Will we love them enough to labor on their behalf when they can return nothing but a stammered "thank you" or a feeble handclasp? Will they continue to love and serve us when our zest for life is drained and we are a hollow shell of our once vibrant selves?

Who can help us best?

Those who are qualified by vocation and training is an important part of the answer. This brings us to part of the bane and blessing of modern times. The blessing is that modern equipment, modern training, and modern technical skills have saved many lives, prolonged others, and kept still others more comfortable on the way to death. All these accomplishments are gifts of God. He is Lord of technology as well as everything else. Chemistry, surgery, and electronic testing are possible only because of the way He has designed the world. And the capacity of our researchers to discover medical breakthroughs is possible only because of the way He has designed the researchers.

Their help then is a blessing in which God's hand is apparent. Yet the way in which that help comes is sometimes a bane. It is usually found only in hospitals and clinics, so we have to venture away from home to find it. It usually comes in a highly supervised system so that visits are limited, personal contact is fleeting, and regulations are strict. Much of that system with its dripping tubes and blipping screens tends to disorient the patient and disenchant the visitor. Hospitals need to work extra hard to bring comfort even while they use all available means to bring healing.

Who can help us best?

Those who have the ability to comfort is the final part of the answer, the part on which the Bible has the most to say: "Blessed be the God and Father of our Lord Jesus Christ, the Father of mercies and God of all comfort, who comforts us in all our affliction, so that we may be able to comfort those who are in any affliction, with the comfort with which we ourselves are comforted by God. For as we share abundantly in Christ's sufferings, so through Christ we share abundantly in comfort too" (2 Cor. 1:3-5).

These magnificent words speak first of the *source* of true comfort. Notice that God is called "the Father of mercies and God of all comfort." Mercy toward the pitiful and comfort for the sufferer are what God has in large measure. Saving and healing are His ministry.

We should also not miss what Paul has said about the *means* of true comfort. Suffering is the way God brings comfort to us: He "comforts us in all our affliction, so that we may be able to comfort those who are in any affliction." No affliction, no comfort. That is the basic law. Out of our suffering comes experience with the God of comfort in whose name we pass on comfort to others.

The *chain* of true comfort we might call this. In His mercy God links together the lives of His sufferers in such a way that one helps the other. How great it is that a caring God wants to waste no experience of suffering. Instead as the Artisan of mercy He uses suffering as the anvil on which to forge His links of comfort.

Who can help us best? A team of healers is what we often need: loved ones to lift the load of our daily cares; physicians, nurses, and technicians to apply the best of modern learning in the fight to relieve pain and encourage life; spiritual persons like chaplains, pastors, and deacons to minister out of their own experiences of suffering and with the comfort that God alone can give.

How Can They Help Us Best?

The question of how they help is huge and its answers vary from case to case.

They can all help us best if we tell them what we need. Nothing is more frustrating than to try to help patients who are so tied up in their own problem that they cannot make the effort to communicate their needs.

For the sake of our loved ones and ourselves we need to be as open as possible about what is going on inside us. When we hurt physically we should make that known to the medical staff. They are best equipped to ease our distress or to help us understand why they cannot ease it.

Where our distress centers in cares about home or job or loved ones, we must share those cares with those who want to help. Even when the needs are beyond the ability of those who want to assist us, we can find some relief by getting the matter off our chest.

When our problems are spiritual, then the persons with spiritual gifts are the ones to confide in. Do not hesitate to talk with the chaplain or your pastor about your anxieties. They can help you know that Jesus is your Saviour and that your sins are forgiven. They can speak to you about the comforts of heaven and the hope of resurrection. They can pray with you about your concerns for the spiritual welfare of those you leave behind.

Our attendants, our loved ones, and our spiritual counselors can help us best, if we let them be less than perfect. Illness and its care set up special stresses. Hospitals are busy and demanding places, often short of staff. Doctors and nurses are only human beings, technically trained but still human. They will try their hardest, but we will hurt them and frustrate ourselves if we expect perfection.

Friends and family, too, are under a great deal of strain. Our illness and the possibility of our death may tie them up in knots. They may not hear all that we say and may not behave as we want them to. Can we have the grace in such circumstances to grant them room to work out their grief and anxiety without feeling that they have failed us or, worse still, that they are somehow responsible for what has happened?

We live by grace as Christians. Can we learn to die the same way? Can we extend God's comfort and compassion to those who are spending themselves to help us?

If our trust in the "Father of mercies and God of all comfort" is strong, we shall be able to comfort those who comfort us. All of us want to stay as fully alive as possible until God calls us home. The best way to do that is to demonstrate mercy and compassion toward those who minister to our needs. As we do, we can count on the best kind of help from them and from God who makes all true comfort possible.

4. How Much Should I Fear Death?

Since therefore the children share in flesh and blood, he himself likewise partook of the same nature, that through death he might destroy him who has the power of death, that is, the devil, and deliver all those who through fear of death were subject to lifelong bondage. For surely it is not with angels that he is concerned but with the descendants of Abraham. Therefore he had to be made like his brethren in every respect, so that he might become a merciful and faithful high priest in the service of God, to make expiation for the sins of the people. For because he himself has suffered and been tempted, he is able to help those who are tempted.

Hebrews 2:14-18

41

He was as superstitious as anyone I had ever met. He had been raised in the rural south and had moved to California just after World War II. I was a young college student filled more with curiosity than with compassion at the time, and I used to pry at his fears with hypothetical questions.

Death was his most feared taboo. "If you lost your wallet in a cemetery and it had $10,000 in it, would you go back at night to fetch it?" His answer came with no hesitation: "It would either be there in the morning, or it would not be there at all!" Not even the threat of losing $10,000 would move him to venture into the realm of the dead after dark. In fact, it would have taken forceful pressure to get him there during the day.

His was an extreme, an exaggerated case of what most of us feel. The subject of death makes us uncomfortable. It is not a subject that we readily turn to for easy conversation, like the baseball scores, or the latest count of our grandchildren.

It is a more sobering, a more somber topic than any of those. And it is to be handled in hushed and dignified terms. We talk of it only when someone close to us dies or when death holds the headlines in disaster—like the tragic plane collision in the Canary Islands that killed nearly six hundred persons. When the subject enters the room we are prompted to stand at attention and place our hands over our hearts in solemn salute.

The power, the strangeness and even the terror of death produce a sense of awe within us. We can probably state that even more frankly: we are afraid of death—afraid of the subject and afraid of our own dying.

And with some good reason. Death is an intruder that charges into the circle of our lives, breaks up its fellowship by snatching someone from us, interrupts our plans and projects, and forces us to face our most frightening limitations. Death wrenches spirit from flesh with a force and finality that leave us baffled, angry, and fearful. One moment there is a living, breathing, feeling human being by our side, and the next moment there is a pale, still, silent shell. We cannot quite understand what has happened, and fear is surely one of our reactions.

Part of our fear may be this: death forces us to look into a mirror. The funeral of a friend is a prophecy of what will happen to us. A lonely shudder rattles through our bodies as we think of it. The tolling of the funeral bell is for each of us.

The Feelings that Feed Our Fears

The uncertainty of death is a feeling we all share. Who of us knows exactly what happens? What will it feel like? Will I feel anything? Will I know what is going on?

The reports of persons who have been close to death and returned to tell their stories are of some help. They often speak of their consciousness of separation from their bodies. They tell of looking down on the hospital scene with its flurry of doctors and nurses scrambling around the bed or the operating table. The dying person has become a spectator at his own death and has watched the scene peacefully from above it all.

Some of this is comforting. Persons who have been through that experience profess not to fear dying as they once did. But the rest of us have not had that privilege, and the uncertainty of how it feels to do something as permanent as crossing from this world to the next remains with us.

The frustration of death is another feeling we can readily understand. Death is not courteous. Its timing often seems less than thoughtful. Sometimes it takes the loved one who seemed physically strongest and leaves the more dependent partner behind for others to care for. That is frustrating. Sometimes it takes people at the height of their power when they have reached the point of maximum productivity. Kenneth Strachan was one of the great missionary strategists of our day, general director of the Latin America Mission. Hodgkins disease snatched him from among us just at the point when his international leadership was beginning to be recognized in the church.

It was the same with Paul Little. Tragically he died in an automobile accident just when he was launching his career as an outstanding teacher and writer in evangelism at Trinity Evangelical Divinity School. His death left plans unfulfilled and projects uncompleted. We find this frustrating and somewhat fearful. It may well happen to us. I had a friend who always cleared his desk at night in case he died before morning. But none of us can really do that. Death virtually always catches us in mid-sentence and leaves us with endeavors half done.

The dread of judgment is another feeling that feeds our fears. "It is appointed for men to die once, and after that comes judgment" (Heb. 9:27). Those stern words from the New Testament are an awesome summation of the relationship between death and judgment. It is the reality of judgment that lends death part of its terror.

Some of this biblical message is lost on our society. We are so time-bound and so earth-oriented that we blissfully ignore the possibility of judgment. But it is there, one of life's great realities. The Creator who launched our lives on the choppy seas of history will call us to account for the quality of our seamanship.

Finally, we feel the threat of annihilation when we contemplate our dying. We look in the mirror and say, "What will happen to all of this corporate and spiritual self, this sculpted, moving pile of tissue and soul? Will I be gone?" A very portly friend of mine was ordered by his doctor to lose 150 pounds. In dismay he looked at himself, felt his flabby flesh, and lamented "What will I be like when half of me is

45

gone?'' Double the anguish of that question and you have an inkling of how the threat of annihilation chills us, when we think of death.

The Faith that Fights Our Fears

How much should I fear death? There is no simple answer to that question. Our response depends on what we fear about death and why we fear it. The answer is personal. Each of us fears different things about death and to differing degrees.

More than anything else, our fears vary according to how much we trust God. Research shows that doctrinal belief, intellectual acceptance of biblical propositions is not enough. The doctrine needs to sweep into our lives and change our attitudes. Where there is strong personal faith, fear of death will diminish; where there is not, fear of death will increase.

It is *faith* that fights our fears. To help us in this fight, in fact to rescue us in the midst of it, was one reason why Jesus came: "Since therefore the children share in flesh and blood, he himself likewise partook of the same nature, that through death he might destroy him who has the power of death, that is, the devil, and deliver all those who through fear of death were subject to lifelong bondage" (Heb. 2:14,15).

The uncertainty we fear about death can be decreased by the assurance that Jesus understands. Just earlier the author of Hebrews reminded his hearers that Jesus "is not ashamed to call them [His people] brethren," because we, like Him, are sons of God (Heb. 2:11). Our frailty, our mortality, our concern about death are not foreign experiences to the Son of God, who shares our flesh and blood. The Lord who walks by our side along the path that leads to death—and life—has walked that way before. He did not become an angel, who is not subject to death; He became a mortal human being. With the wisdom and poise of a pioneer leading new settlers through unfamiliar terrain, He knows all the twists and turns. Because He is the Light of the world He guides us through death's darkness with full assurance. "For because he himself has suffered and been tempted, he is able [as a merciful and faithful high priest in the service of God] to help those who are tempted," including those of us who are tempted to fear death more than we need (Heb. 2:18).

The frustration we fear about death can be diminished by the promise of sharing Jesus' glory. This is God's ultimate answer to our problem of feeling interrupted in our efforts, incomplete in our human service. Bargaining for more time is something most of us are eager to do as our stay on earth grows short. So much seems to be left undone.

Yet it is Christ's perfection that is the key. His suffering and exaltation are the path to perfection, the route that God chose for Christ to demonstrate His complete obedience and to lift us to the place of glory in God's presence. Listen again to the words from

47

Hebrews: "For it was fitting that he [God], for whom and by whom all things exist, in bringing many sons to glory, should make the pioneer of their salvation [Jesus] perfect through suffering" (Heb. 2:10). Jesus' suffering was the path to His perfection, as God's obedient Son, fully doing the Father's will. It was also our road to glory.

Glory and perfection—what can these mean but that God's plans will be perfectly carried out and God's people will not be frustrated by what is undone, but thoroughly satisfied. When faith tells us that glory—fulness of blessing at God's side—is our inheritance, we need not fear the frustration that death allegedly entails.

The judgment we fear in death can be abolished by the certainty that Jesus is the Saviour. Here the key word is not often used in modern parlance—expiation. We hear it in this sentence: "Therefore he had to be made like his brethren in every respect, so that he [Jesus] might become a merciful and faithful high priest in the service of God, to make expiation for the sins of the people" (Heb. 2:17). Who could be our priest before God but the Lord Christ who became one with us? No mere angel, no vague spirit could hold our needs before God, only the Man who had tasted of suffering and death on our behalf. As our divine-human Priest, He is able to make expiation, that is to offer a sacrifice that will turn aside God's judgment and make His forgiveness possible.

48

What a heroic act! With one great deed of love, our Saviour has rescued us from the fear of judgment by bearing that judgment for us. Death is real; death is awesome; but its ultimate terror is broken. History's Judge has a smile on His face for all who can trust Him for their forgiveness.

The annihilation that we fear in death can be defeated by the confidence that we are children of God. "Here am I, and the children God has given me" (Heb. 2:13) is what the risen Christ proclaims. We belong to Him. We are sons and daughters of the eternal and living God. Can any power snuff out our lives and turn us into nothing? Not sin. It has been forgiven. Not the devil. He has been destroyed by Christ's death. His power is broken. The Lord of life reigns supreme, and we are His. That is what our faith tells us.

Can we believe? Can we let our biblical affirmations become so much a part of us that fear is put to flight by the power of faith in a living God? We will not relish death, but neither will we dread it. We may not want to traipse through cemeteries at night, but we will no longer be plagued by superstition. We will see our lives linked to the love of God and we will trust that love to death's door—and beyond.

5. What Happens at Death?

For we know that if the earthly tent we live in is destroyed, we have a building from God, a house not made with hands, eternal in the heavens. Here indeed we groan, and long to put on our heavenly dwelling, so that by putting it on we may not be found naked. For while we are still in this tent, we sigh with anxiety; not that we would be unclothed, but that we would be further clothed, so that what is mortal may be swallowed up by life. He who has prepared us for this very thing is God, who has given us the Spirit as a guarantee.

51

So we are always of good courage; we know that while we are at home in the body we are away from the Lord, for we walk by faith, not by sight. We are of good courage, and we would rather be away from the body and at home with the Lord. So whether we are at home or away, we make it our aim to please him. For we must all appear before the judgment seat of Christ, so that each one may receive good or evil, according to what he has done in the body.

2 Corinthians 5:1-10

The outward symbols of death are well known. A *cemetery* is not hard to detect, especially a traditional type with upright tombstones and marble crosses. A *hearse* is rarely confused with any other vehicle. Its style and shape sets it apart from all other emergency equipment—ambulances, patrol cars, and rescue vans. A *coffin* is like no other box, whether the plain wood coffin, mummy-shaped with shoulder space slightly wider than head or foot, or the rectangular satin-lined casket with brass handles. No container for tools or machinery looks quite like a coffin.

These outward symbols tell us that we are in the presence of death. But they do not tell us much else. The mystery of what happens at death will not be unraveled by meditation in a cemetery, investigation of a hearse, or reflection on a coffin. They are all part

52

of the visible, tangible world which, though real, is transient, as the apostle Paul pointed out: "So we do not lose heart. Though our outer nature is wasting away, our inner nature is being renewed every day. For this slight momentary affliction is preparing us for an eternal weight of glory beyond all comparison, because we look not to the things that are seen but to the things that are unseen; for the things that are seen are transient, but the things that are unseen are eternal" (2 Cor. 4:16-18).

The signs of our wasting away in our outer nature are highly visible in the gnarled knuckles of our arthritis, the increased thickness of our spectacle lenses, the attachment of hearing aids to our glasses—and finally in the cemeteries, hearses, and coffins that punctuate the end of our story on earth. These are the expressions of "our slight momentary affliction." We can all see them and know what they mean.

But none of these signs tells us the full story of death. They tell us nothing about "an eternal weight of glory beyond all comparison," for which our earthly suffering—especially our suffering for the sake of Christ—prepares us. The things that truly count, the things that last to eternity, are unseen. We can only know them by faith. What happens behind the scenes at death is one of these unseen realities. Just watching it will not tell us what we yearn to know. It is to God who alone can see the unseen that we go for better information.

Three great realities about death are among the lessons He can teach us as Christians. First, death has given way to sleep. Second, death will lead to wholeness. Third, death is crowned by fellowship. All the human eye can see are the destructive effects of death—a painful end, a deteriorating even decomposing body, a ruptured circle of fellowship. All of these are real. Death is often fraught with pain. Our bodies do return to dust. Our family units are wrenched apart. But more happens than those three apparent experiences. The death and resurrection of Jesus have made possible other, less visible, realities which are even more real than what we see.

Death Has Given Way to Sleep

One of these realities has to do with death itself. Its nature has been changed so drastically that Paul has even changed its name: "But we would not have you ignorant, brethren, concerning those who are alseep, that you may not grieve as others do who have no hope. For since we believe that Jesus died and rose again, even so, through Jesus, God will bring with him those who have fallen asleep" (1 Thess. 4:13,14). Twice he used the term *sleep* to describe the state of death for Christians.

In so doing, Paul followed his Master's lead. You remember how Luke described the scene at Jairus' house, when his servant brought the report that Jairus' daughter had already died: "And when he

54

[Jesus] came to the house, he permitted no one to enter with him, except Peter and John and James, and the father and mother of the child. And all were weeping and bewailing her; but he said, 'Do not weep; for she is not dead but sleeping.' And they laughed at him, knowing that she was dead" (Luke 8:51-53).

The disciples and Jairus' family knew the outward, visible signs of death. Squeeze as they would the girl's wrist they could wrench no pulse from it. Squint as they did at the mirror held over her silent lips they could detect no moisture. Pulse and breath had ceased, sure signs of death. What they did not know was the difference Jesus' presence made. With Him by their sides, death had given way to sleep. The unseen power of God was even more real than the very real evidence of death.

For those who trust what Christ can do, death is no longer permanent. It is a sleep from which we will awaken. He is resurrection and life. His power to defy death by raising the dead—not only Jairus' daughter, but Lazarus and the son of the widow of Nain—and by His own resurrection make it impossible for death to have a permanent grip on Christ's people. The stranglehold in which death clutched us has been broken and death itself has been pinned to the mat.

For those who believe that Christ is Lord, death is no longer terrifying. Who is afraid to lie down and sleep! It is harmless at worst and refreshing at best.

Jesus' death and resurrection have made the difference. "For since we believe that Jesus died and rose again..." was the way Paul began his argument. Note that he did not use the term *sleep* to describe *Jesus'* death. He used the cold, blunt, harsh word *died.* Jesus was spared none of death's terrors. In fact His death was about as brutally frightening as any you can imagine. Sheer torture we should call it— with mockery, cruelty, even savagery in the heavy cross, the harsh whip, the biting thorns, the jagged nails, the puncturing spear.

But because He died that death and rose again, death looks different to those who believe. Robbed of its permanence, stripped of its terror, it has been rendered as harmless as sleep. Its outward signs may show us wasting away; its inward truth, its eternal reality seen by faith's eye, is that it is preparing us for resurrection and renewal.

Death Will Lead to Wholeness

One of the things that we dread about death is that it seems to diminish us, to make us less than what we are. Even the process that leads to death is often one of shrinkage. We lose weight, we are bent over, our skin and flesh seem to shrivel, we have less hair and fewer teeth. Virtually every bodily function slacks off in its efficiency. We struggle in the face of such reduction to cling to full selfhood. Our egos wane to the point where they scarcely cast a shadow. Those are the transient realities that human eyes can see.

But with death, as with all spiritual reality, it is what the eye cannot see that truly counts. Here are Paul's words which describe how death will lead to *wholeness* not *dissolution:* "For we know that if the earthly tent we live in is destroyed, we have a building from God, a house not made with hands, eternal in the heavens. Here indeed we groan, and long to put on our heavenly dwelling, so that by putting it on we may not be found naked. For while we are still in this tent, we sigh with anxiety; not that we would be unclothed, but that we would be further clothed, so that what is mortal may be swallowed up by life. He who has prepared us for this very thing is God, who has given us the Spirit as a guarantee" (2 Cor. 5:1-5).

These are mind-boggling and faith-stretching words. They tell us that what happens at death is not at all what appears to happen.

God will fulfill our longing for wholeness. Our sighs and our groans, as we labor under the fraility of a failing body, an earthbound tent, are not our last words. Our last words will be eternal praise for the renewal and restoration that God will work when He gives us that other body—a building not a tent, divinely given not handmade, eternal in the heavens not destructible on earth.

As we watch our human tent fray, unravel, and split at the seams, we feel our personhood seeping out and running away. Nakedness is what we fear, according to Paul, the anxiety that we will be embarrassingly unclothed. Incomplete, unwhole, lacking in some essentials of personality—those are the dreaded adjectives with which we fearfully describe our future. "Away with all of that!" was Paul's exhortation. Death will lead to wholeness. Paul's announcement was exuberant in its hope—"what is mortal may be swallowed up by life." That summed it up. *Life* is the unseen reality, the eternal state for all who believe. And that life is poised to pounce on all that is mortal about us and to swallow it as a cat would a canary.

God has given His Spirit as a guarantee of wholeness. The new life is not only on the way; it is already here. The Spirit of God who works within us is the Spirit of life, of renewal, of resurrection. As He tells us of God's love, as He instructs us in God's ways, as He tutors us in God's will, He is preparing us for the life to come. He is leading us toward the wholeness that will ultimately be ours.

God's commitment to us is neither fragile nor fickle. He is totally serious about making us new. And He has sent His Spirit as the seal of that seriousness. The Spirit is like God's down payment on our full salvation. Having sent His Spirit to start the work, He intends to follow through on the entire transaction.

Death Is Crowned by Fellowship

What happens at death? What we can see is the least important part. Death has given way to sleep,

58

and death will lead to wholeness. By faith we affirm these great realities.

And one more: death is crowned by fellowship.

Death is a form of homecoming. "So," Paul wrote, because we have God's Spirit in us as a pledge of our future wholeness, "we are always of good courage; we know that while we are at home in the body we are away from the Lord, for we walk by faith, not by sight. We are of good courage, and we would rather be away from the body and at home with the Lord" (2 Cor. 5:6-8). We cannot lose, Paul claimed. When we are in the body here on earth, we walk by faith knowing that God is in us and knowing what He has ahead of us. Good courage is our disposition. Death is the only thing that can change that. And it changes our lives for the better. Faith gives way to sight; fellowship with God at a distance is replaced by fellowship in God's presence. What happens at death? Death brings the Christian home.

Pleasing God is our aim in life and death. "So whether we are at home or away, we make it our aim to please him" (2 Cor. 5:9). There is something more important than life or death. In fact we could call it a matter of life and death. Doing God's will in worship and love is what life is about. That is our work on earth; that will be our task in heaven.

The cemetery, the hearse, the coffin—by them we are reminded regularly of our mortal frailties. Can we see beyond them? Can we see those other eternal realities that tell the full story of death? Can we see the basic differences Jesus has made in robbing death of its sting? And can we live all of life for the will of Him who has made that eternal difference for us?

6. What Has Christ Done About Death?

*Do not be ashamed then of testifying to our
Lord, nor of me his prisoner, but take your
share of suffering for the gospel in the power
of God, who saved us and called us with a holy
calling, not in virtue of our works but in
virtue of his own purpose and the grace
which he gave us in Christ Jesus ages ago,
and now has manifested through the appearing
of our Savior Christ Jesus, who abolished death
and brought life and immortality to light
through the gospel.   2 Timothy 1:8-10*

There is something missing from most modern
cemeteries. Lavish green lawns sprawl over un-
dulating hillsides. Marbled mausoleums glisten like
the Taj Mahal in the morning sun. Wrought iron
gates open on spacious drives. But there is still
something missing.

Some of these cemeteries boast beautiful flower
gardens that make them attractive to tourists. Others

house art and sculpture with the glory of a Renaissance palace. Where I live, cemeteries are among the great show places—right along with the Queen Mary in Long Beach, the observatory at Mt. Palomar, or Disneyland—where we take our mid-western cousins. Yet something is missing in modern cemeteries.

The manicured greenery is so undisturbed by funeral monuments that you have to look twice to distinguish a cemetery from a golf course. The office has the warmth and welcome of a country club but something is not quite right.

There are no crosses. The flatly laid, uniformly chiseled headstones are depressed in the lawn and only visible to those who venture out to visit the cemetery plots. Ease in maintenance has taken priority over truth in theology. The lawn mower has come to outrank the Bible.

A pity this, if not a tragedy. The cross is missing from the field of death. The sign of comfort and life has all but disappeared from the arena where it represents the best hope of victory.

With death we need all the help we can get. Its mystery shadows us all of our lives and often keeps us from enjoying what we are and have. That ominous future hangs its question marks like black crepe from all our doorknobs. No religious faith, no spiritual experience can be significant in the long run that does not help us deal with death.

There can be no saviour, no bringer of hope, no

rescuer from despair who does not give us perspective on our dying. Easy optimism, sugarcoated advice, syrupy answers to hard questions all stick in our throats when we come to face that last reality.

That is why the cross is so important. It is the sign that Jesus is an expert in the matter of dying; it is the credential that validates His right to give us help. More than a doctor's diploma on his wall, more than a policeman's badge on his chest, more than a judge's gavel on his bench, the cross of Jesus shows that He is licensed to aid us with our dying.

What has Christ done about death? A legitimate question that is. If He is to be our Lord and Saviour then He has to prove Himself capable in our area of dire need. What has He done? How has He made a difference in our dying? How has He transformed the experience which we know to be unavoidable? Three simple affirmations may sum up Christ's credentials in the subject of death: (1) He has felt its pain with us; (2) He has borne its judgment for us; (3) He has broken its hold over us.

He Has Felt Its Pain with Us

Heroics are singularly absent from the story of Jesus' life. The focus is on His simple humanity and His total dependence on God. Where miracles are worked they are not to make Jesus larger than life but to witness to the presence of God's power. Where His teaching is profound its purpose is to make clear the

63

will of God, not to elevate the teacher.

Nowhere is the simple humanity of His incarnation more clear than in the events that precede His death. His is a powerful story, simply and directly told in the Gospels.

He knows the loneliness of death. It is an experience that no one else can fully share. One of His friends turned him over to the enemy; another would not acknowledge His friendship; others forsook Him to save their own necks. The Roman procurator washed his hands of any involvement; the Jewish rulers refused to intervene; the sons and daughters of Jerusalem abandoned Him in mockery. His disciples slept while He anguished. What can be more lonely than a cross? Lifted up beyond the reach of human compassion, isolated from the touch of friends, Jesus died. A strange crew comprised the deathwatch: Roman soldiers and convicted thieves. Only His mother and one close friend stood vigil by Him, and they were beyond His reach. With us, Jesus has felt the pain of death.

He knows the anguish of death. Most death is painful and would be even more so but for the medical relief now available in more civilized places. Probably crucifixion is as excruciating as any way of dying we can think of. It is slow and hard. Hands and feet sting from the biting of the iron pegs and the tearing of the fragile flesh. Bones are pulled from sockets and sinews are jerked from their moorings by the weight of the hanging body. Life slowly ebbs as bleeding and dehydration sap the strength. Add the ignominy and the despair, and the combination is heartrending. Jesus has felt the pain of death.

Its loneliness and anguish were no strangers to Him. He spent an anxious night and a harrowing day getting acquainted with them. But because He did, death looks different to us. The One we love and trust has been there first, God in human flesh has walked its rocky road, drunk its bitter cup, immersed Himself in its fearful baptism. We can take heart. Christ has done something about death—He has felt its pain with us.

He Has Borne Its Judgment for Us

The cup Jesus drank, the cup He asked to be removed from Him, was more than loneliness and anguish. It was judgment. Cup often means that in the Scriptures:

> On the wicked he will rain
>   coals of fire and brimstone;
> a scorching wind shall be
>   the portion of their cup.
> (Ps. 11:6)

What Jesus wrestled with in the garden was the terror of judgment: He was to shoulder our sins. This was a terrifying experience. Think how the weight of our sins crushes us to the breaking point. What would it be like to sit in a room with all the people who had ever known you and to hear them recount one by one all the wrong things that you had ever said or done? You would melt like wax under that pressure. Now multiply that experience by the number of persons who ever have lived, are living, and will yet live and you can get an idea of Christ's burden. No wonder He begged the Father to take away that cup, so deadly and so full. It was the cup of judgment He was drinking for us.

What Jesus struggled with on the cross was again the horror of judgment: He was separated from the Father. Human language has no more painful cry than these words which Jesus wailed in His agony: "My God, my God, why hast thou forsaken me?" (Matt. 27:46). The woes of the world were heaped upon Him. The One who knew no sin was made sin for us. The judgment of separation from God which we had earned He embraced. He bore the judgment of death for us.

And both of these experiences were new to Him. Their novelty added to their terror. Neither sin nor separation had been part of His life. Righteousness and fellowship were His constant companions. The judgment of death took Him where He had never been and gave Him what He had not deserved.

And death for the rest of us has never been the same. That cross, that instrument of execution, has become the judgment stand. The crucifixion scene is the chamber of history's supreme court.

There Jesus bore our judgment, paid our fine, took the death penalty in our place. Whatever else may make us anxious about death, judgment need not contribute to our anxiety. The cross is God's great word of pardon to those who hope in His mercy.

He Has Broken Its Hold over Us

What has Christ done about death? The cross is one part of the answer to that question. On the cross He looted death of its strangeness and plundered it of its judgment. But He was not through with that last enemy. The scene around the cross at three o'clock on that dark Friday afternoon seemed heavy with defeat. The friends were wracked with guilt; the mother was bent with grief; the lifeless body was ready for the wrapping. A Roman crucifixion had claimed another victim; a potential rebel had received His just deserts.

That was Friday. By Sunday morning the whole picture had changed. Grave clothes were neatly folded in the borrowed tomb. The stone stamped with the official seal had been rotated away from the opening. The grave site was as empty as it had been two days before.

Death had been defeated. God's resurrecting power had gone to work. The last enemy became the loser.

Death has never been the same. It is a reality, of course. Only in rare circumstances do we welcome it.

We respect its power, its surprises, its timing. We do not fear its terror.

We are the winners, not death. Christ by His cross and empty tomb has broken its hold over us. Beyond our dying stands the power of God to make us whole again. We need not doubt about the future; the risen Lord is already there calling us to it. He shows *His* resurrected body as the guarantee of *ours*.

Our modern cemeteries have it wrong. Manicured lawns, marble sculptures, tidy headstones, plush slumber rooms are not the answer. Momentary comfort, temporary ease is all they afford. The old symbols are still the best. Nothing will speak to our fear, uncertainty, and grief more than they.

A cross has a message to shout in the ear of death itself. Jesus knows and cares about our dying; He has been through it. Jesus wants us to escape the wrath of judgment; He gave up everything to make that possible. Jesus offers resurrection life beyond the barrier of death; He himself breached that wall and opened the way for complete victory.

What has Christ done about death? Everything possible to lead us through it with power and dignity. The wonder of Jesus' work is best celebrated in this joyful summary of what He was done for us:

> But take your share of suffering for the
> gospel in the power of God, who saved us
> and called us with a holy calling,
> not in virtue of our works but in virtue

of his own purpose and the grace which
he gave us in Christ Jesus ages ago,
and now has manifested through the appearing
of our Savior Christ Jesus, who abolished
death and brought life and immortality
to light through the gospel.
(2 Tim. 1:8-10)

7. Does Death Have the Last Laugh?

But in fact Christ has been raised from the dead, the first fruits of those who have fallen asleep. For as by a man came death, by a man has come also the resurrection of the dead. For as in Adam all die, so also in Christ shall all be made alive. But each in his own order: Christ the first fruits, then at his coming those who belong to Christ. Then comes the end, when he delivers the kingdom to God the Father after destroying every rule and every authority and power. For he must reign until he has put all his enemies under his feet. The last enemy to be destroyed is death. "For God has put all things in subjection under his feet." But when it says, "All things are put in subjection under him," it is plain that he is excepted who put all things under him. When all things are subjected to him, then the Son himself will also be subjected to him who put all things under him, that God may be everything to every one.   1 Corinthians 15:20-28

Death does not seem to be a humorous topic. Most of the time our conversations about it are hung with somber crepe and edged in black. We begin them with words like, "So sorry to hear" and "Please accept my sympathy."

Laughter is scarce at funerals. Shouts of joy are rarely raised in cemeteries. Morticians seem to smile less than the rest of us. Death is tinged with seriousness. What place has humor, where suffering has been so keen and the sense of loss so vexing?

Death does look serious when we stand close to it. It is grim and hard to laugh at. If there is any laughter in the face of dying, death seems to be doing it. We feel mocked and jeered by the insufferable ways of death.

What the Bible helps us do is to step back and look at death from a little distance. The better perspective gives us a glimpse of another side—we can almost call it a lighter side—of death. There is a form of humor called *irony* and that brand of humor provides a lens through which we can gaze at death—and laugh. My *Webster's New Collegiate Dictionary* gives this as one definition of irony: "Incongruity between the actual result of a sequence of events and the normal or expected result." Irony is a biting surprise, a sudden twist of circumstances by which winners become losers and vice versa.

The stories of Joseph and Esther provide good examples. Joseph's brothers plotted to get rid of him

72

because he was their father's favorite. They sold him to a slave caravan headed for Egypt. (See Gen. 37:18-28.) "Good riddance," they boasted. "Now we do not have to deal with him any further." What a surprise they received years later when they trudged to Egypt for relief from famine, only to discover that the governor whom they begged for grain was their despised brother. Irony, this was—incongruity between what they expected and what actually happened.

The experience of Haman in the book of Esther has been a source of subtle humor to all who have read it for 2000 years and more. Haman, a high official in the Persian court, could not stomach Mordecai, an old Jew who refused to pay Haman the homage which the Persian thought appropriate. Haman's hostility built to the point of murder: he ordered a gallows to be constructed for Mordecai. Beyond that he secured an edict from the king that sentenced to death all Jews in the realm. By a twist of providence, Mordecai saved the life of the king by warning him of a plot to assassinate him. Only later, when Mordecai was about to be executed did the king realize who had saved his life and order Mordecai to be honored. (See Esther 3-6.)

The king sought Haman's advice about the honor without telling him whom it was for. Haman, puffed with pride, assumed that the honor was for him. Glowingly he described all that should be done to honor an illustrious hero: the king's robes and horse, a parade through the city square, a herald calling the attention of the citizens to the royal honor. "Good," said the king. "Do all of that for Mordecai!" The irony of it all stung Haman speechless. His despised enemy was to bask in royal glory. That irony turned grim when Queen Esther, Mordecai's niece, saw to it that Haman's treachery was exposed, and he was hanged on his own gallows.

The story of Jesus' battle with death is filled with that kind of irony. We can almost hear the hosts of heaven chuckle as the plot unfolded. Paul, in his great sermon on the Resurrection (1 Cor. 15), traced the progress of the irony.

Death Has Changed to Sleep

"But in fact Christ has been raised from the dead, the first fruits of those who have fallen asleep" (1 Cor. 15:20). There is more than a little humor in the term "fallen asleep." As we have already seen, this was Paul's way of showing that the permanence and the terror of death had been replaced by a temporariness and a peacefulness akin to sleep.

We take "fallen asleep" as a figure of speech. Paul was not teaching a doctrine of "soul-sleeping" in which believers have a period of quiet unconsciousness while they await their resurrection. He was merely describing the way in which death's sorest pangs—its finality and its fear—had been removed

74

by Christ's death and resurrection. Christians can face death with composure, knowing that the power of Christ has turned it into an experience no more permanent and no more dreadful than sleep.

Christians have the last laugh. Even the fearsome enemy who has stalked us the length of our lives can be handled. Death is a toothless tiger, a beaten dog whose bark is worse than its bite. Those believers whom it holds in its clutches are not so much dead as asleep—so at home are they with God, so certain is their hope of resurrection.

Death Is Conquered by Resurrection

"For as by a man came death, by a man has come also the resurrection of the dead. For as in Adam all die, so also in Christ shall all be made alive" (1 Cor. 15:21,22). Can you imagine how baffled and battered death would have been as it heard those words? One resurrection was bad enough. Death lost its shining prize when God raised Jesus from the dead. But now, the promise was given that *all* the dead would be raised. Christ's resurrection was the guarantee—"the first fruits" Paul called it—of the rest of the crop. As the early heads of ripening grain hold promise for an abundant harvest so Christ's resurrection is the assurance of a great resurrection yet to come.

Part of the irony of this is that it comes in connection with the human family. The same human nature that in Adam blazed a trail into sin, death, and judgment will pioneer a path to forgiveness, life, and fellowship. We should not miss the humor. It is through the man Christ Jesus, not through angels or spirits, that God brought resurrection. Human beings are good at dying. We all know that. Who would have guessed that a human being, a man, would also be champion of resurrection. You can almost hear the angels laughing at the empty tomb. The tables had been turned on death. The cemetery, death's domain, had been invaded by the power of God working in a mortal man. It was a surprise worth smiling over. And still is.

Death Is Robbed of Its Supports

Death has enjoyed the help of some henchmen in its agelong reign of terror. Paul mentioned them when he pictured the end of history that will be brought about by Christ's second coming: "Then comes the end, when he [Christ] delivers the kingdom to God the Father after destroying every rule and every authority and power. For he must reign until he has put all his enemies under his feet. The last enemy to be destroyed is death" (1 Cor. 15:24-26).

Those henchmen have high-sounding names: rule, authority, power. They are the spirits that unbelieving and superstitious persons fear. They are the demonic forces that play on our human fear of death. They get us to ignore death so as not to face its reality or to become obsessed with it so that life loses meaning.

Magic, witchcraft, astrology, sorcery, spiritualism are their realm. They distort our view of death so that we fail to trust God to help us cope with it.

But they too are doomed. Their lofty labels will not save them on judgment day. Their fate is already sealed. Paul was speaking of God's great work, "which he accomplished in Christ when he raised him from the dead and made him sit at his right hand in the heavenly places, far above all rule and authority and power and dominion, and above every name that is named, not only in this age but also in that which is to come" (Eph. 1:20,21). As high as those spirits might be judged to be by the superstitious followers, Christ has risen above them.

Death's strong supporters have more than met their match. The fear and foolishness with which these demon powers infected the mass of humanity are no longer necessary. We can back off and laugh at their coming impotence. The all-powerful Christ has the might and the authority to deal with them. Their very names—rule, authority, and power will ring with irony—when the last trumpet sounds. To God and to no one else in earth, hell, or heaven belong the kingdom, the power, and the glory.

Death Is Replaced by Another Kingdom

The final touch of irony has to do with that kingdom. In contrast with death, Christ the new victor is not grabby. He has no need to keep the winner's trophy for Himself. As Son and Servant of God, He has labored in the power of His Father and according to the Father's will.

This is why He won, not death. He had not His own success in mind but the completion of the Father's plan. It was that subservience, that dependence, that humility which God used and blessed.

Nowhere does Christ's royalty show itself more than when He hands the kingdom—won by His obedient life, His selfless death, and His dramatic resurrection—back "to God the Father after destroying every rule and every authority and power" (1 Cor. 15:24). Can we feel the irony here? Death fought desperately to retain its kingdom by putting Jesus to death and by that very act began to lose it. Jesus won the kingdom by not wanting it for Himself and by being ready to deliver it to God the Father.

No longer is death's kingdom sovereign. Its end is assured and already in sight. The mighty battles of crucifixion and resurrection have assured its doom. The time is at hand when "God may be everything to every one" (1 Cor. 15:28). All other masters will be set aside, shorn of their crowns, and God's lordship will be celebrated throughout the universe.

Can you sense the freedom that all this means? Freedom for you? If you have trusted in Christ as living Lord and gracious Saviour, you have the freedom to view death as sleep and to face it with composure. If you believe that God raised Jesus from the dead, you have the freedom to treat death as a conquered enemy. Whatever damage it may seek to do has been overcome by the power of resurrection. If you can realize that magical fears and demonic superstitions have been destroyed by the risen and ascended Lord, you have the freedom to look at life and death through clear eyes, unblurred by the absurd and irrational things most people dread. If you can enter into the hope of God's new kingdom, then you have the freedom to worship and serve Him without fear of horrible failure or dreadful judgment.

What does the end of death mean to me? It means that in Christ there is a new beginning whose very motto is freedom—freedom to trust, freedom to serve, freedom to hope. It is in that freedom that a Christian can face death not only without nagging fear, but perhaps with quiet laughter. It is death on whom history's last surprise will be played. Then God will do the laughing. I am sure He does not mind if we join His laughter ahead of time.